Beware the Bite!

DEADLY ANIMALS

by Alex Hall

Minneapolis, Minnesota

Credits
Cover and title page, © Byrdyak/istock; 4TL, © bennytrapp/Adobe Stock; 4B, © Ramon Carretero/Shutterstock; 5M, © seread/Adobe Stock; 5MR, © Pluto Mc/Adobe Stock; 6, © Kris Wiktor/Shutterstock; 7, © Mark_Kostich/Shutterstock; 8, © MSK1147/Adobe Stock; 9, © wirakorn/Adobe Stock; 10, © Jay Ondreicka/Shutterstock; 11, © Scott Delony/Shutterstock; 12, © Milan Zygmunt/Shutterstock; 13, © Kevin/Adobe Stock; 14, © Ken Griffiths/Shutterstock; 15, © Timothy Lubcke/Adobe Stock; 16, © Phil Bird/Adobe Stock; 17, © Justin Tyler Barlow/Shutterstock; 18, © Rudi Hulshof/Shutterstock; 19, © Gregor Bogdanski/Adobe Stock; 20, © Tomas Drahos/Shutterstock; 21, © PHOTOCECH/Adobe Stock; 22, © Adalbert Dragon/Shutterstock; 23, © christian vinces/Adobe Stock; 24, © Grigorii Pisotsckii/Shutterstock; 25, © The Nature Guy/Adobe Stock; 26, © Martin Prochazkacz/Shutterstock; 27, © Mohsin/Adobe Stock; 28, © Ken Griffiths/Adobe Stock; 29, © WavebreakMediaMicro/Adobe Stock; 30TL, © priyank/Adobe Stock; 30B, © Will Falcon/Adobe Stock

Bearport Publishing Company Product Development Team
Publisher: Jen Jenson; Director of Product Development: Spencer Brinker; Editorial Director: Allison Juda; Editor: Cole Nelson; Editor: Tiana Tran; Production Editor: Naomi Reich; Art Director: Kim Jones; Designer: Kayla Eggert; Designer: Steve Scheluchin; Production Specialist: Owen Hamlin

Library of Congress Cataloging-in-Publication Data is available at www.loc.gov or upon request from the publisher.

ISBN: 979-8-89577-087-0 (hardcover)
ISBN: 979-8-89577-530-1 (paperback)
ISBN: 979-8-89577-204-1 (ebook)

© 2026 BookLife Publishing
This edition is published by arrangement with BookLife Publishing.

North American adaptations © 2026 Bearport Publishing Company. All rights reserved. No part of this publication may be reproduced in whole or in part, stored in any retrieval system, or transmitted in any form or by any means, electronic, mechanical, photocopying, recording, or otherwise, without written permission from the publisher. Bearport Publishing is a division of FlutterBee Education Group.

For more information, write to Bearport Publishing, 3500 American Blvd W, Suite 150, Bloomington, MN 55431.

Contents

A World of Killer Critters 4
Animals Bite! 6
Mosquito 8
Black Widow Spider 10
Gila Monster 12
Inland Taipan 14
Honey Badger 16
Nile Crocodile 18
Hippopotamus 20
Jaguar 22
Piranha 24
Great White Shark 26
The Deadliest Bite!. 28
Critters Everywhere. 30
Glossary. 31
Index 32
Read More 32
Learn More Online 32

A World of Killer Critters

The world is full of wonderful, wild, and dangerous critters! Animals everywhere have lots of different ways to defend themselves or catch a tasty meal.

Whether an animal looks cozy or killer, it's best to watch out! It might just sting, bite, claw, or squeeze you when you least expect it.

READ ON TO LEARN MORE ABOUT SOME OF THE WORLD'S SCARIEST BITING ANIMALS . . . IF YOU DARE!

Animals Bite!

One of the ways animals stay safe or dig into a tasty meal is to bite. *CHOMP!* But what makes an animal's bite so dangerous?

When some animals bite, their strong jaws and sharp teeth do a lot of damage. Other creatures have pointy fangs that deliver deadly **venom**.

The bites of animals can be dangerous in different ways. They may even pass on diseases that cause sickness or death. And what makes all this biting even scarier? It can happen at lightning speed!

Let's take a look at some killer critters and score their dangerous bites. We'll rate their damage, how fast they move, and if they deliver venom or pass on disease. Which animal will win this deadly competition?

Mosquito

The first competitor is the tiny mosquito. Most people know about this **insect**. Its bite leaves a bump on the skin that can itch for days. But don't be fooled by their small size. Mosquitoes can be deadly!

When a mother of a mosquito is looking for a meal for its young, the insect bites an animal, sucks up its blood, then flies away. But many kinds of mosquitoes also leave behind dangerous diseases.

Mosquitoes around the world spread malaria, yellow fever, Zika, and other illnesses. Nearly one million people die from diseases carried by mosquitoes every year. Yikes!

KILLER CRITTER SCORECARD

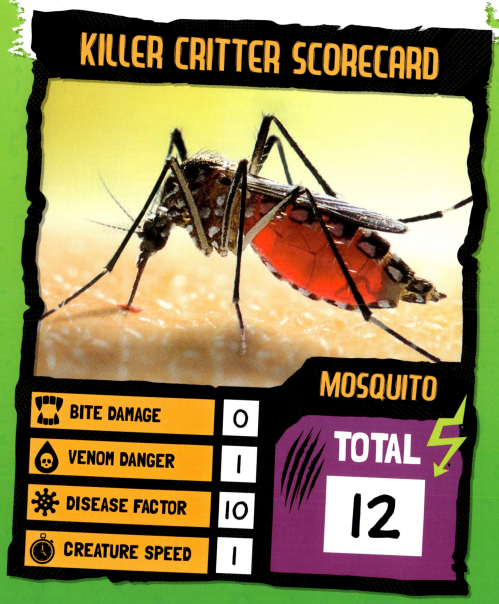

MOSQUITO

BITE DAMAGE	0	
VENOM DANGER	1	
DISEASE FACTOR	10	
CREATURE SPEED	1	

TOTAL: 12

Black Widow Spider

The black widow spider is known for the red hourglass-shaped mark on its **abdomen**. It's also known for a venomous bite.

These spiders live throughout most of the world. They trap insects in their sticky webs before quickly killing them with a deadly bite. Dinner is served!

While these spiders usually leave people alone, a mother black widow will bite humans to protect her eggs. If a healthy person is bitten, they may feel sick. The bite can be deadly, however, to small children or older people. Watch out!

KILLER CRITTER SCORECARD

BLACK WIDOW SPIDER

BITE DAMAGE	1	
VENOM DANGER	8	
DISEASE FACTOR	0	
CREATURE SPEED	3	

TOTAL: 12

Gila Monster

The Gila monster is the largest wild lizard in the United States. Although this **reptile** is fairly slow, its bite packs a punch!

A Gila monster stores venom in the bottom of its jaw. When the creature bites, the venom flows through the animal's sharp teeth and into its victim.

The Gila monster eats mostly eggs and small animals. So, many scientists believe the creature's venom is used mainly to defend itself, rather than to catch **prey**. Although its bite rarely kills humans, it can be very painful.

KILLER CRITTER SCORECARD

BITE DAMAGE	4
VENOM DANGER	7
DISEASE FACTOR	3
CREATURE SPEED	0

GILA MONSTER

TOTAL: 14

Inland Taipan

Inland taipans blend in with their wild homes, ranging in color from dark brown to olive green. While these snakes may not look dangerous, their deadly venom is definitely something to watch out for!

The inland taipan is nicknamed the fierce snake. This reptile lives in the hot, dry parts of Australia and is the most venomous snake in the world.

The inland taipan will generally ignore humans unless it feels **threatened**. If it does, the snake can attack with lightning speed! After its venom passes through its fangs and into its victim, the person can be dead within 45 minutes.

KILLER CRITTER SCORECARD

INLAND TAIPAN

BITE DAMAGE	3
VENOM DANGER	10
DISEASE FACTOR	0
CREATURE SPEED	8

TOTAL 21

Honey Badger

While its name makes it sound sweet, the honey badger is not cuddly! This fearless fighter gets its name from a love of eating honey. To find it, however, the badger will tear open an entire beehive with its razor-sharp claws!

These **mammals** are only about the size of a small dog. However, they have strong jaws, sharp teeth, and extremely powerful bites. Honey badgers are known to rip apart snakes and fight off much larger **predators**, including lions and hyenas.

In addition to being strong and fearless, these critters are also very intelligent. The animals can easily break into hen houses when searching for a chicken dinner. Watch out!

KILLER CRITTER SCORECARD

HONEY BADGER

BITE DAMAGE	10
VENOM DANGER	0
DISEASE FACTOR	0
CREATURE SPEED	8

TOTAL 18

Nile Crocodile

Let's check out this tough-skinned reptile. The Nile crocodile lives in African freshwater swamps, rivers, and wetlands. To catch its prey, it lurks in the water, waiting to suddenly strike.

Once the Nile crocodile bites down, it locks its jaws and quickly rolls over. This so-called death roll can rip apart its victim.

Nile crocodiles have one of the most powerful bites in the animal kingdom. These fierce predators kill hundreds of people every year. Beware!

KILLER CRITTER SCORECARD

NILE CROCODILE

BITE DAMAGE	10
VENOM DANGER	0
DISEASE FACTOR	1
CREATURE SPEED	6

TOTAL: 17

19

Hippopotamus

Although the hippopotamus is a **herbivore**, this large animal isn't afraid of a fight. It is quick to defend its **territory** and has even been known to charge at boats.

A hippo's mouth is huge! The animal opens its jaws wide to scare enemies or prepare for an attack.

Hippos use their very sharp teeth for fighting. They have the strongest bite of any land mammal, thought to be powerful enough to cut a human in half! Up to 3,000 people die every year from hippopotamus attacks.

KILLER CRITTER SCORECARD

HIPPOPOTAMUS

BITE DAMAGE	10
VENOM DANGER	0
DISEASE FACTOR	0
CREATURE SPEED	5

TOTAL 15

Jaguar

When you think of a mouth full of sharp teeth, a big cat may come to mind. The jaguar has the strongest bite of any big cat.

Jaguars are often found roaming the rainforests of Central and South America. These spotted predators blend in with the speckled landscape of their leafy home, easily hiding when hunting prey.

And a jaguar's victim doesn't stand a chance. This big cat's bite is so strong that it can even go through turtle shells! Luckily, jaguar attacks on humans are rare. Still, watch out if you're strolling through the rainforest!

KILLER CRITTER SCORECARD

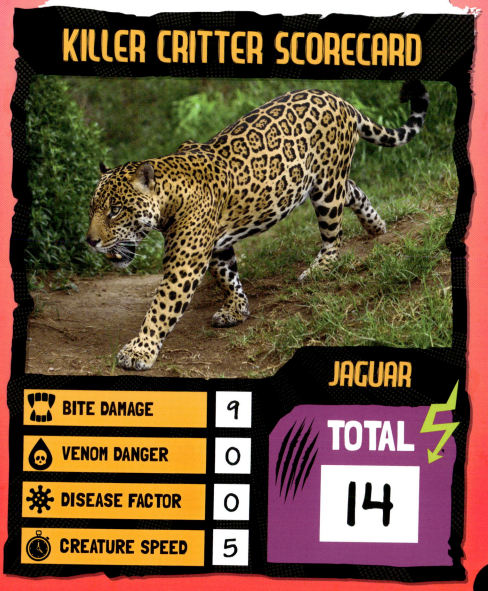

JAGUAR

BITE DAMAGE	9
VENOM DANGER	0
DISEASE FACTOR	0
CREATURE SPEED	5

TOTAL: 14

23

Piranha

Watch out for snappy little fish in the lakes and rivers throughout South America. Piranhas have the strongest bites of any animal their size. And not only are their jaws strong, but their mouths are also full of supersharp teeth!

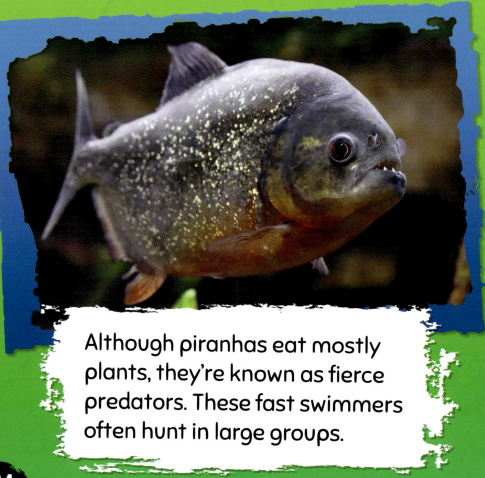

Although piranhas eat mostly plants, they're known as fierce predators. These fast swimmers often hunt in large groups.

When a group finds prey, the piranhas all begin biting and eating at once. With so many fish attacking, the meal is quickly devoured. Attacks on humans are rare, thankfully!

KILLER CRITTER SCORECARD

PIRANHA

BITE DAMAGE	8	
VENOM DANGER	0	
DISEASE FACTOR	0	
CREATURE SPEED	7	

TOTAL: 15

Great White Shark

Beneath the surface of the ocean is a predator that many people fear. The great white shark is famous for its massive jaws, pointy teeth, and huge appetite.

The giant mouth of a great white shark is full of teeth. It has about 50 teeth visible with 5 or 6 rows of new teeth growing behind them.

These toothy predators find prey by following sounds and smells in the water. Then, they attack at super speeds, sometimes even leaping out of the water! The great white is the shark most likely to attack humans, usually mistaking them for seals.

KILLER CRITTER SCORECARD

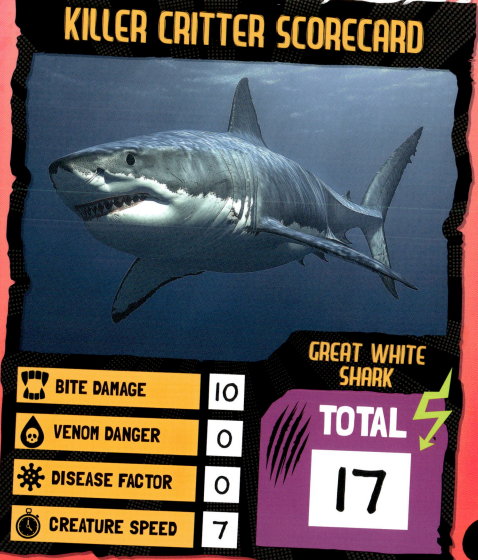

GREAT WHITE SHARK

BITE DAMAGE	10
VENOM DANGER	0
DISEASE FACTOR	0
CREATURE SPEED	7

TOTAL: 17

The Deadliest Bite!

Who comes out on top in this killer critter competition? The inland taipain wins!

While this snake isn't the biggest animal in the competition, its incredible speed and killer venom make it the deadly winner.

A person bitten by an inland taipan would soon feel weak and dizzy. Before long, their **organs** might start to fail. The victim would need help right away!

Luckily, scientists have made **antivenom** for these snakebites. This medicine is given to bite victims to stop the effects of the venom.

Critters Everywhere

The world is a big place, full of amazing animals. But the next time you see a wild critter, beware. It might have powerful jaws, venomous fangs, or pointy teeth!

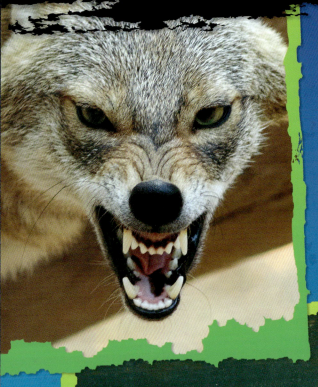

Glossary

abdomen the larger of a spider's two main body parts

antivenom a medicine that blocks the effects of venom

herbivore an animal that eats only plants

insect an animal with six legs, three body parts, and an exoskeleton

mammals animals that have warm blood, a backbone, and that produce milk

organs parts of the body, such as the lungs, that do a particular job

predators animals that hunt and eat other animals

prey animals that are hunted and eaten by other animals

reptile a cold-blooded animal with scales

territory the area where an animal usually lives

threatened in danger

venom a harmful substance that is injected through a bite or a sting

Index

eggs 11, 13
fangs 6, 10, 15, 30
humans 13, 15, 21, 23, 25, 27
insects 8, 10
jaws 6, 12, 16, 18, 20, 24, 26, 30
mammals 16, 21
oceans 26
rainforests 22–23
reptiles 12, 14, 18
skin 8, 18
snakes 14–16, 28

Read More

Golkar, Golriz. *Hippopotamus (Deadliest Animals).* Mendota Heights, MN: Apex Editions, 2023.

Mattern, Joanne. *Super-Deadly Animals (Super-Incredible Animals).* Mankato, MN: Black Rabbit Books, 2025.

Roggio, Sarah. *Crocodiles vs. Hippos: Food Chain Fights (Predator vs. Prey).* Minneapolis: Lerner Publications, 2025.

Learn More Online

1. Go to **FactSurfer.com** or scan the QR code below.
2. Enter **"Beware Bite"** into the search box.
3. Click on the cover of this book to see a list of websites.